強豔花壇ものがたり

著　藤本三和子
写真　三好和義

PHP

まえがき

花を好んだ祖母は、「強羅花壇」で花のかおりのお香を焚いていました。1989年に新生「強羅花壇」をオープンさせ、客室名に花壇の屋号に添って花の名前をつけました。そして、お客様に喜んでいただきたい一心で邁進してまいりました。

館内を移動する際に外気や四季を感じてもらえる「強羅花壇」の象徴でもある柱廊は、日本文化のよさを取り入れたものです。旅行が好きで海外のホテルに泊まった際、これは素晴らしいと感じたおもてなしを日本に置き換えて、どんどん取り入れていきました。

2023年、寂しい気持ちはありましたが、次の世代に「強羅花壇」を継承いただくために、元気なうちにバトンタッチすることを決断しました。そして世代とともに「強羅花壇」の形が変わっていくに際し、私たちがつくってきた軌跡を何かの形にして残したいと考え、本書を著した次第です。あらゆることでお客様に喜んでいただくために全力で取り組む、それが「強羅花壇」のおもてなしの心であり、揺るがない思いです。その心意気を少しでも感じていただければ嬉しいです。

著者

新緑の庭の風景　Garden of vibrant green

Preface

My grandmother loved flowers, and she used to burn flower-scented incense at Gora Kadan. When I unveiled the rebirth of Gora Kadan in 1989, I gave each guest room the name of a flower, a token of the hotel's name. Since then, I have dedicated myself whole heartedly to ensuring the happiness of our guests.

The gallery, used for transitioning between spaces within the hotel, captures the essence of the weather and the changing seasons. It reflects the core values of Japanese culture and symbolizes Gora Kadan, which translates to "the flower gardens of Gora." I love to travel, and after staying at hotels overseas, I transferred and adapted the aspects of hospitality that I found most valuable to fit the cultural context of Japan.

In 2023, though it made me sad, I decided to pass the baton to the next generation, so they could take over management of Gora Kadan while I was still active. And seeing that Gora Kadan is changing with the new generation, I wanted to leave a record of what I made, which led to my writing this book. We do our utmost to make guests happy in every way; this is the Gora Kadan spirit of hospitality, one that will never waver. I hope you feel something of that spirit in these pages.

[目次] Contents

まえがき　Preface — 001

思い出がつまった箱根の地　Hakone, place of memories — 008

美しいものに導かれて　Beauty shows the way — 014

別荘からのスタート　In the beginning there was the villa — 020

イタリア語が運んでくれた新天地　Italian brings me a new world — 024

名旅館を目ざす　Aiming to become a world-renowned Japanese inn — 030

日本の美を大切にしつつ快適な空間を　Comfortable spaces, Japanese beauty — 034

若き建築家との出会い　Meeting with a young architect — 042

こだわったのは「自分が心地いいこと、楽しいこと」　Careful attention to what feels comfortable and enjoyable — 046

無駄な空間の「贅」　Superfluous space embodies luxury — 052

日本の土と技が光る瓦　Tiles that shine with Japanese clay and craftsmanship — 056

宮様の洋館の美しさを今に　Updating the beauty of a Princely Western building — 060

こんこんと湧き続ける源泉　Ever-flowing geothermal springs — 061

伝統職人たちの匠の技を生かして Making the most of the craftsmanship of craftsmen ── 066

季節の懐石料理をこだわりの器で Seasonal traditional cuisine, served on carefully chosen dishes ── 070

花、花、花…… Flowers, flowers, flowers! ── 074

メイド・イン・ジャパン！ Made in Japan! ── 078

着物に込めたおもてなしの心 Hospitality in kimono ── 086

すべてはお客様に喜んでいただくため Everything we do is to please our guests ── 092

おもてなしとは Hospitality accumulates ── 096

人の笑顔を見ることが嬉しくて…… When I see our guests smiling, I can't help but be pleased ── 104

人から人へ評判が伝わって Reputation is transmitted from person to person ── 112

一つひとつの出会いが宝ものです Each encounter is precious ── 113

日本の「おもてなし」の極美を堪能する時間　三好和義（写真家） Experiencing the ultimate in Japanese hospitality—Kazuyoshi Miyoshi, Photographer ── 120

あとがき Afterword ── 124

檜皮葺の玄関　Entrance with hinoki bark roof

思い出がつまった箱根の地

幼い頃から箱根とはご縁がありました。祖父母の別荘がこの強羅にあり、毎年夏になると泊まりがけで遊びに来ていたのです。

別荘は、元々は旧皇族の閑院宮載仁親王が所有されていた館だったそうです。その後はご次男の春仁王が引き継がれましたが、戦後、皇籍を離脱されてこの別邸も手放すこととなり、それを土地ごと譲り受けたのが祖父でした。

約1万坪の広い敷地は、豊かな緑にあふれていました。ところどころにきれいな沢が流れていて、沢ガニがとことこ歩き、生い茂る草花の間を何十種類もの蝶々やトンボが飛んでいます。都会育ちでしたが、自然が大好きだった私にとって、ただ歩き回るだけでも楽しく、心躍る遊び場でした。

お盆になると、正面に見える明星ヶ岳の大文字焼きの火が、漆黒の闇のなかに浮かび上がります。その厳かで幻想的な風景は、今も目に焼きついています。まさか将来自分が、この地で旅館を経営するなど思いもしなかった頃のお話です。

「強羅花壇」の歴史は、ここからはじまりました。

外気を感じる柱廊　Feeling the outside air in the gallery

春のサロン「青嵐」　Salon Seiran in Spring

Hakone, place of memories

Hakone has been part of my life since I was a child. My grandparents' villa was here in Gora, and I used to spend part of every summer with them.

The villa originally belonged to Prince Kan'in no Miya Kotohito of the former Imperial family. His second son, Prince Haruhito, inherited the property, but after the war, he left the Imperial family and had to give up the property. Along with the land, it was granted to my grandfather.

The spacious grounds of over three hectares were lush with greenery, with pretty little streams winding through the landscape, river crabs tapping their way over the stones, and dozens of species of butterflies and dragonflies flitting amid a profusion of flowers and plants. I was a city girl, but loved being in nature. Just walking around the property made my heart leap with joy.

During the summer festival of Obon, the ritual fire that formed the character for "big" on Mt. Myojogatake, which faces the property, glowed in the inky darkness. That solemn, fantastic image is still etched in my memory.

At the time, I would never have believed that someday I would be managing a Japanese inn on this very same plot of land.

This is where the Gora Kadan story begins.

夕暮れどきの玄関路地　Entrance alley at dusk

美しいものに導かれて

幼い頃両親が離婚し、祖父が父親代わりでした。明治生まれの男ですから、甘い愛情表現など苦手な無骨な人でしたが、祖父なりのやり方で私たちきょうだいを可愛がってくれました。

今でも覚えているのは、当時銀座にあった「小松ストアー」という百貨店に、よく私たちや従兄弟たちを連れていってくれたことです。ただし、祖父は「好きなものを買ってきなさい」と言うだけで、付き添いは私の母任せ。自分は車の中にデンと座ったまま「15分で帰ってこい！」などと命令するのですから、なんともせっかちでした。

さて、そんなときのことです。子どもたちが大はしゃぎで「これ買って」とせがむのは、たいてい流行りの玩具や可愛いぬいぐるみです。ですが、私だけは大人の女性がパジャマの上に羽織るような舶来品のガウンなどを選ぶのです。シルクの滑らかな手触りや繊細な刺繍にたまらなく心を奪われてしまうのです。

なぜかはわかりませんが、美しいものがとにかく好きでした。それは、私の人生を貫く「芯」のようなものでした。

中学2年生の冬休みのこと。祖母がヨーロッパ旅行に連れ出してくれました。まだ個人の海外旅行は許されない時代でしたから、数人のツアーを組んでの渡航でした。イギリスのロンドンを出発点に、オランダのアムステルダム、ドイツ、リヒテンシュタイン、スイス、フランス……と南下していく旅は、まさに美しいものとの出合いの連続でした。そして最後に訪れたイタリアで、私は衝撃を受けました。道行く人のファッション、建築物や街並みの美しさはもちろんのこと、言葉では言い表せない何かに魂をわしづかみにされてしまったのです。

イタリアのことをもっと知りたい。現地でイタリア語を学びたい。海外留学はまだ珍しい時代でした。祖父は「女だてらに何を言うか」と反対すると思っていました。ところが実際相談すると、「これから日本はどんどん国際化する。女性でも語学を学ぶことは将来必ずプラスになるだろう」と、賛成してくれたのです。祖父は新潟の片田舎から上京し、きちんとした学問を受ける機会がないまま苦労して自分で証券会社を興した人でした。学ぶことができなかったことを、孫の私に託す気持ちもあったのかもしれません。

通っていた聖心女子学院の短大を卒業した年、私はイタリアのペルージャという小さな街を目指して日本を離れました。19歳でした。

初夏の別邸・日本庭園をのぞむ　View of the villa and Japanese garden in early summer

We arrived in London, from there traveling southward through Amsterdam, West Germany, Lichtenstein, Switzerland, France…it was a series of moments filled with beauty. Our final stop was Italy. Of course, the street fashions, the architecture, and the neighborhoods were stunning, but what truly captivated me was a feeling I couldn't put in words — a deep resonance that touched my soul.

I want to know more about this country. I want to study Italian here in Italy.

At the time, there were few Japanese studying abroad. I thought my grandfather would oppose the idea, saying something like "What are you talking about? You're just a girl." But when I consulted him, he said, "From now on Japan is going to internationalize rapidly. Studying foreign languages will be an advantage in the future, even for women." And so he gave me his blessing.

My grandfather had come from the backwoods of Niigata Prefecture, moved to Tokyo, and with no opportunity for formal education, established a successful stockbroking business through sheer hard work and determination. I believe he may have wanted to give me the chance to study that he had never had.

The year I graduated from University of the Sacred Heart Junior College, I left Japan for a little town called Perugia. I was 19 years old.

Beauty shows the way

My parents divorced when I was young, and my grandfather was like a father to me.

As a man born in the Meiji era, he was rough and unaccustomed to sweet expressions of affection, but he was affectionate to me and my siblings in his own way.

I still remember how he used to take us and our cousins to Komatsu Store, a department store that was then in Ginza. But all he would say was, "Pick out whatever you like," and he left the rest to my mother. "Be back in 15 minutes!" he would order us, while he stayed behind solemnly in the car. He was always impatient.

On these visits to the store, the other children would run around excitedly, begging my mother, "Buy this for me!"—usually a popular toy or a cute stuffed animal. Only I would choose something like an imported dressing gown, something an adult woman might wear over her pajamas. The smooth feel of silk, or delicate embroidery, never failed to steal my heart.

I'm not sure why, but I simply could not resist the allure of beauty. Beauty has always been a guiding light in my life.

It happened during the winter vacation of my second year of middle school. My grandmother took me on a trip to Europe. This was at a time in Japan when international travel by individuals was challenging due to various regulations, so she organized a tour group instead.

別荘からのスタート

強羅の祖父母の別荘では、1952（昭和27）年から旅館業を営むようになっていました。旅館といってもわずか5部屋だけの、プライベートなゲストハウスのようなものでした。喘息の持病があった祖母が、空気のいい箱根に長逗留したいけれど、一人でポツンと過ごすのは寂しいし時間をもてあますからと、お客様をお迎えすることにしたのです。

大がかりな準備も何もなく、手先の器用な祖母が自分でお客様用の浴衣をチクチク縫ったといいますから、そこを「強羅花壇」と名付けました。

花が好きだった祖母は、まさに家庭的な宿でした。祖父も祖母も旅館業には門外漢で、事業を大きくしようという野心もありません。ところが、時は、高度成長期にさしかかったばかり。箱根は熱海と並んで新婚旅行のメッカでもありましたので、お客様は引きも切りません。とにかく客室が足りないからと、請われるままに増築を重ねていきました。実際の運営はその道のプロにお任せして、なんとか切り盛りしていたのが実情だったようです。

020

夕暮れ時の柱廊　Colonnade at sunset

春の夕暮れに別邸の庭をのぞむ
Looking into the garden of the villa at dusk in spring

In the beginning there was the villa

In 1952, my grandparents were managing an inn at their villa in Gora, though with only having five guest rooms it was more like a private guest house. My grandmother had long suffered from asthma, and she preferred to remain in Hakone, where the air was pure. But it was lonely by herself, and with time on her hands, she decided to take in guests.

No major modifications were made to the villa, and my grandmother, skilled in handcrafting, sewed the guests' cotton kimonos herself. It was a truly cozy place to stay.

My grandmother loved flowers, and she named the inn Gora Kadan.

Neither of my grandparents knew anything about running an inn, and they had no ambitions to expand the business.

Yet, in that era, Japan's economic miracle was just getting under way, and Hakone ranked along with Atami as a favorite honeymoon destination, which helped ensure that the inn was always full. There never seemed to be enough guest rooms, and new construction was always in progress. My grandfather and my grandmother turned the day-to-day operation of the inn over to professionals, and somehow they managed to keep things on track.

イタリア語が運んでくれた新天地

ペルージャで学んでいた私のもとに「祖父が脳溢血で倒れた」という連絡が来たのは、イタリア語をなんとかマスターした頃でした。
このまま祖父と会えなくなってしまったらどうしよう……。不安と心配で、週に1便しかなかった日本行きの飛行機を待つのももどかしく、取るものもとりあえず帰国の途につきました。

幸い祖父は一命を取りとめたものの、そこからは長い闘病生活がはじまりました。祖父をおいてまたイタリアに戻るわけにもいかず、これから何をしようかと、一時は途方に暮れていました。

時は1970年代。ちょうどイタリアの文化が日本に入ってくるようになり、ファッション、食材、医薬品などの商品市場が開かれはじめたばかりでした。この新しいビジネスチャンスにさまざまな企業が名乗りをあげましたが、そのとき必要になったのが、商談に立ち会える通訳者の存在でした。

そこで、どういう経緯か白羽の矢が立ったのが、私でした。

024

私程度の語学力でお役に立てるのだろうかと不安でした。ただ、当時はイタリア語ができる人がほとんどいなかったからでしょう。予想外にたくさんのご依頼をいただき、それから3年間ほどは忙しい日々が続きました。

そんな折り、知人を介してアルファキュービックというファッションメーカーから「うちに来ませんか？」とお声がかかりました。

まだ創業したばかりでしたが、最先端のファッションやカルチャーの発信源として時流に乗り、飛ぶ鳥を落とす勢いで成長していた会社です。聞けば、新しくイタリアのファッションを扱っていきたいので、手伝ってほしいとのこと。美しいものが好きだった私にとって、とても光栄で嬉しいお誘いでした。はじめての会社員という立場に戸惑いもありました。ですが、何度もイタリアに出張させていただき、当時イタリアンファッションの最も華やかな時代の幕開けであり、まだ日本で知られていないブランドを開拓したりする毎日は楽しく充実したものでした。

「これから日本はどんどん国際化する」と言った祖父の言葉は本当でした。あのときイタリア語を学ばせてもらったことが、私の人生にさまざまな可能性を開いてくれたのです。

祖父は、そんな私の姿を見届けるようにして他界しました。

春の別邸・「曙」の露天風呂　Open-air bath at Akebono villa in the spring

Italian brings me a new world

I was studying in Perugia when I received news that my grandfather had suffered a stroke. By this time I had somehow managed to master Italian.

What if I never saw my grandfather again? I was so anxious and worried, I could barely endure the wait for the one flight to Japan each week, but the day arrived at last, and I set off for home.

Fortunately my grandfather was still with us, but it marked the beginning of a long struggle to regain his health. I couldn't very well leave him and go back to Italy, but I was at a loss for what to do next.

This was the 1970s, just around the time Italian culture had begun to enter Japan, and markets for products like apparel, food, and pharmaceuticals were beginning to open up. Many companies were looking with increasing interest on this business opportunity, but what they needed was interpreters who could sit in on business discussions. And somehow, they found me.

I wondered whether my language skills would be good enough to be of use. But at the time, there were almost no Italian-language interpreters. Perhaps because of this, I received many more jobs than I had expected, and for three years or so I was busy every day.

庭の桜を見上げる　Looking up at cherry blossoms in the garden

Then one day, an apparel manufacturer named Alpha Cubic, which had heard of me through an acquaintance, invited me to join them.

The company had only recently been launched, but it was growing at a blistering pace, riding cutting-edge trends in fashion and culture. They told me they wanted to get into Italian fashion, and they wanted my help. For someone drawn to beautiful things as I happened to be, I was honored and delighted by the invitation.

I was very nervous, this being my first corporate job. But I was able to visit Italy frequently on business at a time when the curtain was rising on Italian fashion's most glamorous era. Everyday was rewarding and satisfying, especially as I uncovered brands that were previously unknown in Japan.

My grandfather was right when he said, "From now on Japan is going to internationalize rapidly." By making it possible for me to study Italian, he opened up many new possibilities in my life.

It was as if he had been waiting until he knew I was safely on my way, then my grandfather left this world.

名旅館を目ざす

祖父が私に遺してくれた「強羅花壇」をどうするか？　大きな選択を迫られました。

当時の私は、アルファキュービックから独立し、イタリア関係のレストランやジュエリーのプロデュースをやってみないかとのお話をいただき、将来の夢を描いていました。旅館業をやるつもりはなかったし、そもそも何の知識も経験もない私などに女将が務まるはずもありません。売却という選択肢もあったのですが、そのとき脳裏に浮かんだのが、幼い頃から大好きだった、あの強羅の美しい自然でした。

「駅から近くて温泉も湧いている。あんな素晴らしい場所を今手放してしまったら、次に買いたくなっても買えませんよ」との周囲の声もあり、考え込んでしまいました。

そんなとき、相談にのってくださった古巣アルファキュービックの社長さんが、ぶっきらぼうですが、こんな言葉をくださいました。

「着るものだけがファッションじゃない。人のライフスタイルにかかわることすべてがファッションなんだ。三和子、日本一の旅館をつくってみろよ」

このひと言が、私の迷いを吹っ切ってくれました。

別邸の庭の春を感じる　Experiencing spring in the garden of the villa

柱廊は強羅花壇の象徴でもある　　The gallery is the symbol of Gora Kadan

Aiming to become a world-renowned Japanese inn

What to do with Gora Kadan, which my grandfather left to me? I had to make a major decision.

At the time, I was presented with the opportunity to leave Alpha Cubic and become an independent consultant specializing in Italian-themed restaurants and jewelry while also contemplating my future ambitions.

I had no intention of pursuing the inn business; to start with, I had none of the expertise or experience I would need to manage an inn. Selling the property was an option, but in the back of my mind, I could see the beautiful Gora scenery I loved as a child.

People told me, "It's close to the station, and you have a hot spring. If you let go of that wonderful place, you won't be able to buy another like it." I couldn't decide what to do.

I asked the president of Alpha Cubic what I should do. Rather brusquely, he gave me the following advice.

"Fashion isn't just clothing. Fashion permeates every facet of people's lifestyles. Miwako, make Gora Kadan the best inn in Japan."

His advice dispelled all my doubts.

日本の美を大切にしつつ快適な空間を

祖母がそうだったように、オーナーになるだけで実際の運営はプロにお任せすることもできたでしょう。ですが、生来好奇心が強く、一からモノをつくるということに対する興味や情熱は人一倍ありました。

やるからには、みなさんに本当に喜んでいただけるような旅館をつくりたい。

そう考えた私は、「強羅花壇」をそのまま受け継ぐのではなく、新築して、まったく新しい旅館を誕生させようと決意しました。

元々旅が大好きでした。海外のさまざまな国々の素晴らしいホテルに泊まったときの感動は忘れられません。あの素晴らしさに、日本の伝統的な〝和〟のエッセンスが加わった素晴らしい宿を創りたい。そうした思いが、新しい旅館づくりの発想の原点となりました。

アルファキュービックで働いていた時代、毎月のように海外からいらっしゃるたくさんのVIPを接待させていただきました。

当時はまだ東京近郊に高級旅館が少なく、わざわざ新幹線に乗って京都の老舗旅館

にご案内したものです。

その度に、外国人のお客様の反応を見て気づいたことがありました。

たとえば、いくら和の趣が素晴らしくても、身体の大きな外国人にはお風呂が小さかったり、日本式の引き戸であっても、やはりお部屋の鍵はちゃんとかかるほうが安心です。ちょうど日本でもマンションが増えはじめ、私たち日本人も洋風の暮らしに慣れてきた頃でした。これからは日本旅館であっても、ホテルのような快適性や機能性、プライバシーやセキュリティーの確保などが必要になってくるでしょう。

「旅館とはこうであるべき」という概念にとらわれない宿があってもいい。古きよき日本の美意識と意匠を大切にしつつ、とにかく、すべてのお客様に心地よく過ごしていただける空間づくりを目指しました。

こんな発想ができたのも、私自身が旅館業のイロハも知らないまったくのシロウトだったからだと思っています。

幸いマネジメントに詳しい夫が全面的に協力してくれることになり、そこからは二人三脚でのチャレンジがはじまりました。

新緑の「葵」の外観　Exterior of Aoi surrounded by vibrant greenery

Japanese person. The room doors were often traditional Japanese sliding doors, which normally did not have locks, but foreign guests preferred doors with locks. This was around the time that condominiums were becoming widespread, and we Japanese were getting more used to Western lifestyles. I realized that even a Japanese inn would need to offer the comfort, functionality, privacy and security of a hotel.

There was no need for a Japanese inn to be restricted by fixed ideas of what an inn should be.

My aim was to create an inn that showcased the traditional Japanese sense of beauty and design, but above all, one that was designed with spaces to allow all of my guests to be comfortable.

I believe I was able to devise this concept because I myself was a complete amateur who didn't know the first thing about the inn business.

Fortunately my husband, who was well-versed in management, agreed to support me fully. From then on, we faced the challenges of creating the new inn together.

Comfortable spaces, Japanese beauty

On becoming the owner of Gora Kadan, I could have followed in my grandmother's footsteps and left the management of the inn to professionals. But I am curious by nature and passionate about building things from the ground up.

If I was going to do it, I wanted to create an inn that would make people truly happy.

In that case, I thought, I would not take over Gora Kadan as it was. I would rebuild from the ground up and create a completely new inn.

I always loved to travel. I'll never forget the excitement I felt when staying in wonderful hotels in different countries. I wanted to take that excitement, combine it with the essence of traditional Japanese culture, and create a wonderful inn. This desire served as the foundation for conceiving the design of the new inn.

When I worked for Alpha Cubic, I arranged hospitality for many international VIPs almost every month.

At that time, there were few luxury inns in the Tokyo area, so I personally accompanied our guests on the bullet train to Kyoto's established inns.

Whenever I did, I noticed things from observing the reaction of our foreign guests.

For example, no matter how wonderfully Japanese the inn was, the baths were too small for our foreign guests, who were often physically much larger than the average

強羅の自然を感じる　Feel the nature of Gora

客室から大文字山をのぞむ　View of Mt. Daimonji from guest room

若き建築家との出会い

最初のハードルは、建築家をどなたにお願いするかということでした。すでに名のある先生にご依頼する方法もあったでしょう。けれども、私と夫のなかには、すでに「こういうものをつくりたい」という確たる理想がありました。お任せするのではなく、私たちの思いを一緒にカタチにしていってくださるような方を求めていました。

そんななかめぐり会ったのが、竹山聖さんを頭に4人の建築家たちの「設計組織アモルフ」でした。後に30年以上毎年のように行ってきたリニューアル工事の設計を担当してくださった荻津郁夫さんもメンバーの一人でした。

まだ若く世に出ていませんでしたが、皆さん東京大学を出て、知識と才能、情熱にあふれ、お話しさせていただくうちに私たちはすっかり意気投合しました。

参考になりそうな旅館やホテルに実際みんなで泊まってみて、「こんなところがいい」「ここは改善の余地あり」などとアイディアを出し合ったこともあります。後述しますが、当時としては突拍子もないような私の思いつきにも「それ、いいですね！」と賛同してくださるなど、仕事は和気藹々と進んでいきました。

「欅」の中から秋を感じる　Feeling autumn from inside Keyaki

別邸の庭の紅葉をのぞむ
A view of the autumn leaves in the garden of the villa

Meeting with a young architect

Our first hurdle was choosing an architect. We could have turned to a well known architect, but my husband and I already had a firm vision of what we wanted to build. What we needed was an architect who would work with us to realize our concept, rather than someone to whom we would have to entrust the design.

We were therefore fortunate to find Kiyoshi Sey Takeyama, who was then leading a group of four architects in a design group called Amorphe. One of those architects was Ikuo Ogitsu, who for the next 30 years would design the remodeling we carried out almost every year.

At the time, Takeyama-san and his partners were young and relatively unknown, but they possessed remarkable expertise, talent and passion. As we got to know them better, we discovered that we were completely aligned in vision and mindset.

We stayed at inns and hotels that inspired us, taking note of their strengths and weaknesses, and engaging in idea-sharing for improvement. As I will mention later, some of my ideas that seemed crazy at the time were met with enthusiasm, and the effort proceeded harmoniously.

こだわったのは「自分が心地いいこと、楽しいこと」

建築家・竹山聖さんと設計を練っていたときのことです。「あっ」と思い出したことがありました。

それは1979年、新婚旅行で訪れたカリブのホテルでのこと。あちらでもまだあまり見当たらないようでしたが、泊まった部屋にプールがついていました。プールといっても本当に小さくて、泳ぐどころか、ポチャンと入ったら、それでおしまい。冗談で「これがお風呂だったらよかったのにね」と夫と笑い合ったことがあったのです。

そこでひらめいたのが、「部屋に露天風呂があったっていいじゃない」という発想でした。当時は温泉旅館といえば大浴場が一般的でした。ですが、部屋に温泉、しかも露天風呂があれば、いつでも好きな時間に外の景色を眺めながらゆったりとお湯につかれます。大浴場に慣れない外国人のお客様にも気に入っていただけるのではないでしょうか。

実際、1989（平成元）年に新生「強羅花壇」がオープンすると、露天風呂付きの客室の存在は、大きな話題となりました。以来全国にこのスタイルが広がっていき

046

ました。"冗談から駒"のような思いつきでしたが、たいへんありがたいことに「強羅花壇」がパイオニアになってしまったというわけです。

同様に、私たちが先駆けとなったものが、フィットネスジムやスパ（トリートメントルーム）の併設でした。とりわけスパは、タイ・プーケットの『アマンプリ』など海外のラグジュアリーホテルで取り入れはじめたばかりで、日本ではまだあまり知られていませんでした。私自身、お客様から教えていただいたのが最初で、実際行ってみて体験し、その素晴らしさを知りました。

よいと知ったらすぐに「やってみよう」というのが私のモットーです。スパはオープン1年目にベッド1台、セラピスト1人からはじめて、おかげさまで大好評をいただき、本格的にスパとして数名のセラピストとともに始動していきました。

日本旅館といえば、麻雀、カラオケ、指圧が"三種の神器"といわれた時代、そのすべてに背を向け、私自身が「こうなったら楽しいな、心地いいな」と思うことだけにこだわりました。それがお客さまに喜んでいただけることだと信じたからでした。

うちへの融資を担当した銀行の方は、「これで本当に成功するのだろうか？」と、さぞやきもきされたことでしょう（笑）。

047

離れの「花香」の露天風呂　Open-air bath at Kakou

In the same way, we were the first onsen inn to offer a fitness gym and a spa treatment room. Foreign luxury hotels like Amanpuri in Phuket, Thailand were just beginning to introduce spas, and they were still not widespread in Japan. I myself learned of the concept from a guest, so I went and experienced it, and realized how wonderful they were.

My motto is, if something is good, I want to try it myself. During its first year, the spa had one treatment bed and a single massage therapist. Thanks to our guests, the spa was very popular, and we went on to launch full-scale spa services with multiple therapists.

Back in those days, mahjong, karaoke, and shiatsu massage were the three essentials for a Japanese-style inn. I turned my back on all three, focusing on what I myself thought would be enjoyable and comfortable, because I was convinced that our guests would be pleased.

The banker who was funding our construction asked me, "Are you sure this approach will really succeed?" He was very nervous!

Careful attention to what feels comfortable and enjoyable

While we were refining the plans for the inn with Mr. Takeyama, I suddenly remembered something.

In 1979, my husband and I traveled to the Caribbean for our honeymoon. Our room had its own pool, which at that time was still as uncommon in the Caribbean as it was elsewhere. It was truly tiny, not even big enough to swim in, just enough to relax in. We joked that our "swimming pool" really ought to have been a hot spring bath — an onsen.

This, however, sparked the idea of offering each guest room its own open-air rotenburo bath. At the time, onsen inns usually offered a single large communal bath for women and another for men. But a room with its own hot spring bath — a rotenburo bath, outdoors — would allow guests to relax and take the waters while enjoying the scenery any time of the day or night. I also thought that foreign guests, who were unfamiliar with the conventions of Japanese common bathing, would enjoy the rotenburo concept as well.

Sure enough, when the new Gora Kadan opened in 1989, its guest rooms with open-air baths generated considerable interest. And the concept soon spread throughout Japan. It was an idea "from the mouths of babes," but I was very pleased to see Goran Kadan become a pioneer in this sense.

無駄な空間の「贅」

銀行員をやきもきさせたといえば、柱廊もその一つでした。

柱廊は、「強羅花壇」を象徴するようなパブリックな場所で、ロビーから月見台まで約120メートル続く、壮大なガラス張りの列柱空間です。

「ただの廊下」と思えば、確かにお金を生まない無駄なスペースかもしれません。

けれども、廊下は古来、日本の伝統建築になくてはならないものでした。廊下を渡って他の部屋へ行く途中、人は、暑さ寒さの季節を感じます。花鳥風月に親しみ、そこで一句詠むなど、人生の物語が生まれました。「強羅花壇」の柱廊も、そんな日本ならではのドラマチックなスペースでありたいと願いました。

昼は柔らかな太陽の光が差し込み、両側のガラス戸をすべて開け放てば心地よい自然の風が吹き渡ります。月見台からは、春はしだれ桜、夏は新緑、秋は紅葉と季節の彩りを楽しめます。

無駄のなかにこそ風情があり、くつろぎや楽しみがあるのです。

2 階客室からの庭の夕景
Evening view of the garden from a guest room on the second floor

外気を感じる「あじさい」の風呂
Taking in the outside air from the bath at Ajisai

— Superfluous space embodies luxury —

The gallery was one of the things that made our banker nervous.

The gallery is a public space and a symbol of Gora Kadan, featuring a majestic, glassed-in colonnade that runs for about 120 meters from the lobby to the moon viewing platform.

If you think of it as nothing more than a gallery, it is indeed a superfluous space that produces no revenue.

But galleries have always been an essential element of traditional Japanese architecture. As you transition between rooms along the gallery, you can sense the changing temperatures of the outdoors weather's warmth or chill. You can enjoy the beauties of nature, perhaps compose a haiku to describe them, a page from your life story. I wanted the gallery at Gora Kadan to be a dramatic space that was quintessentially Japanese.

By day the gallery is filled with gentle sunlight. Open the glass doors on either side and soothing natural breezes flow through them. From the moon viewing platform you can enjoy the colors of the seasons: weeping cherry blossoms in the spring, the vibrant greenery of summer giving way to the rich reds and golds of autumn.

In superfluity one can find elegance, comfort, and enjoyment.

日本の土と技が光る瓦

瓦といえば屋根瓦を思い浮かべる方が多いかと思います。「強羅花壇」では、その瓦をタイル状にした「敷瓦」をロビーや床に敷きつめました。製作してくださったのは、国内有数の瓦の産地、兵庫県淡路島で活躍されている、瓦作家の山田脩二さんです。今でこそ「敷瓦」は製品化されていますが、当時は、初の試みでした。それを一枚一枚手焼きしてくださったのですから、頭が下がります。

土から生まれた瓦は、自然が持つ柔らかさと力強さを兼ね備えています。墨のようになめらかな光沢があり、周囲の情景をほのかに映します。控えめでありながら品格があり、まさに和の心を凝縮したような美しさです。

この瓦の廊下を歩くのに市販のスリッパでは、あまりにも風情がありません。そこでわざわざ特注で畳草履をつくったのも、私の思い入れの一つでした。草履の底はエコにも配慮した廃タイヤのゴム製で、滑りにくく、お客様にも好評です。

他にも館内には、山田さんの手による瓦アートや古い鬼瓦のオブジェがあり、建物のポイントになっています。

瓦作家・山田脩二さんの手による瓦　Tiles made by tile artist Shuji Yamada

箱根の自然をのぞむ「菊」の風呂
Enjoying Hakone's nature from the bath at Kiku

Tiles that shine with Japanese clay and craftsmanship

Say "tile" and many Japanese will likely think of roof tiles. At Gora Kadan, we laid tile in the lobby and other floor areas.

The person who assisted us was Shuji Yamada, a tile artisan from Awaji Island in Hyogo Prefecture, one of Japan's foremost tile-producing regions. Floor tiles are now commonplace, but at the time it had never been tried before. Mr. Yamada fired each tile individually, a truly impressive achievement.

Tiles born from clay possess a combination of natural gentleness and strength.

They possess a smooth, inky sheen that subtly reflects their surroundings. They are understated yet elegant, with beauty that conveys the real essence of the Japanese spirit.

Because I felt that walking on these titles in conventional indoor slippers would be to miss their true elegance, I had straw tatami sandals made specially to order. Their soles are crafted from environmentally friendly recycled tire rubber for traction, and are popular with guests.

Mr. Yamada also created tile art objects that serve as points of interest in the inn, such as old demon-head ridge-end tiles.

宮様の洋館の美しさを今に

祖父が譲り受けた閑院宮様の別荘は、1930（昭和5）年に建てられた洋館でした。急勾配の切妻屋根と白い塗り壁、木造の梁や柱が外観に出ている、ハーフティンバー様式といわれるものだそうです。

内部は、1階は食堂と応接間、2階はメインのベッドルームとその続きの日本間。廊下をはさんで、宮様の秘書の方用のお部屋という間取りでした。日本間は、宮様の時代には書斎として使われていたようですが、私たちが遊びに行くと、祖母がそこに布団を敷いて寝かせてくれました。幼い頃の楽しい記憶がたくさんつまっています。

旅館のリニューアルに際し、なんとかここを残したくて、洋館建築に詳しい東京大学の藤森照信教授に復元していただきました。

それが今、「懐石料理 花壇」と姿を変えてお客様をお迎えしています。

宮さま時代の調度品は、祖父母の時代、ほとんどを宮内庁にお返ししたと聞きます。でも、内装は、当時のままのモダンなアールデコ様式です。お客様には昭和レトロの洒脱を味わっていただけるのではないでしょうか。

こんこんと湧き続ける源泉

「強羅花壇」が誇れるものの一つに源泉掛け流しの温泉があります。

湯釜は、ヒノキや青森ヒバ。それに、お部屋によっては、巨大な石をくり抜いた露天風呂にもお入りいただけます。

これは、巨石の名所といわれる中国・福建省厦門（アモイ）から採掘してきた自然石を一つひとつ選び、運搬業者の方から「これ以上重いと、もうクレーンでは持ち上がりません」と言われたほど迫力ある佇まいです。

強羅の温泉は、大涌谷や早雲山からの引き湯が一般的ですが、「強羅花壇」は、祖父の代に温泉のボーリングに成功し、敷地内に2カ所の源泉があります。おかげで、箱根一帯の群発地震で、大涌谷界隈の源泉から一滴も湯が出なくなってしまったときも、うちだけは普段と変わらず温泉を楽しんでいただくことができました。

温泉だけでなく、大雨で周辺のみなさんが浸水被害に遭われるなか、この敷地だけスルスルと水がはけていったこともありました。

何か大きな力に守っていただいているのだなと感じます。

自然を感じられる大浴場の露天風呂
Enjoying the surroundings from the open-air bath in the communal baths

Updating the beauty of a Princely Western building

The villa my grandfather took over from Prince Kan'in no Miya included a Western-style building that was constructed in 1930. It was built in the half-timbered style, with a steeply pitched gabled roof, white painted walls, and exterior wooden beams and pillars.

A dining room and drawing room occupied the first floor. The second floor had a master bedroom leading into a Japanese room. There was a room across the hall for use by the prince's secretary. The Japanese room was apparently used as a study in the prince's day; when we visited as children, it was where my grandmother laid out bedding for us to sleep. For me, the house was full of pleasant childhood memories.

When we were rebuilding the inn, I wanted to preserve the Western building somehow, and asked Professor Terunobu Fujimori of The University of Tokyo, an expert on Western architecture, to restore it.

Today, the house welcomes guests as Kaiseki Restaurant Kadan, serving traditional Japanese cuisine.

I believe that most of the prince's household effects and furnishings were returned to the Imperial Household Agency in my grandparents' day. But the interior preserves its original art deco style. We think our guests will enjoy the stylish Showa retro setting.

Ever-flowing geothermal springs

Gora Kadan is proud to have generously flowing geothermal springs.

Guest room interior baths are constructed from Japanese cypress, and depending on the room, guests may also have their own open-air rotenburo fashioned from a scooped-out boulder.

These natural boulders were quarried in Xiamen in China's Fujian Province, an area known for its giant stones, and selected specifically for Gora Kadan. The transport company complained that they wouldn't be able to use a crane if the stones got any heavier. That is how large they are.

Geothermal waters in Gora are usually piped in from Owakudani or Mt. Soun, but well boring during my grandfather's day was successful, and there are two hot springs on the property. Due to this, after a series of earthquakes in the Hakone region, when not a drop of water could be drawn from Owakudani, Gora Kadan's guests enjoyed the waters as usual. And when heavy rains caused extensive damage elsewhere, the water drained quickly away from our site.

I sense that a powerful force is watching over us.

伝統職人たちの匠の技を生かして

 美しいものが好きなこと、海外でよいものをたくさん見たこと。この2つが私を助けてくれました。女将としては少々頼りなくても、家具やインテリアのことなら自分なりのこだわりがあり、一つひとつを自分の目で選んでいきました。
 特に、2021（令和3）年に改築した、別邸「曙」と「暁」は、内装もそうですが、4人位で入れるような大きな庭を眺める露天風呂、専用の内庭の先には芝生の庭園が広がり、奥に連なる箱根の山々は四季折々の彩りを見せてくれます。お客様には、ここで過ごすだけで極上の日本的な体験をしていただけるのではないかと思います。
 こうした伝統的な室礼や庭は、昔ながらの職人さんの手によるものですが後継者不足が深刻です。この強羅にもかつては建具屋さんがあったのですが、お父様の代で店終いしてしまわれました。お願いできる職人さんがいなくて、急きょフロントスタッフが障子の張り替えをしたこともありました。失われゆく日本の文化をせめてこの「強羅花壇」だけでもなんとか守っていきたい。そんな思いが日増しに強くなっていきます。

別邸・「暁」の露天風呂からの庭園
The garden from the open-air bath at the villa Akatsuki

Making the most of the craftsmanship of craftsmen

I love things of beauty, and have discovered many beautiful things on trips abroad.

These two things were helpful to me. Even if I was somewhat lacking as an inn proprietor, I had my own preferences when it came to furniture and interiors, and I selected everything after first seeing it with my own eyes.

The culmination of this approach is reflected in our detached suites, Akebono (Dawn) and Akatsuki (Sunrise), which were renovated in 2021. I chose the interior fittings, and each villa has an open-air bath that looks out on a spacious garden and can accommodate up to four people. A lawn extends beyond the private inner gardens, and the Hakone Mountains, layer upon layer, stretch into the distance, displaying their vibrant seasonal hues. We believe that guests can have an exquisite Japanese experience from such a setting alone.

These traditional room furnishings and gardens were created by experienced craftsmen, but the shortage of successors to carry on these crafts is a serious problem. Gora once had its resident carpenter, but the business had to close for lack of a successor. With no one with the traditional skills to call on, we once had to put inn staff to work replacing the Japanese paper on sliding doors. As Japanese cultural heritage gradually diminishes, I hope that at least Gora Kadan will be preserved. I feel this more strongly every day.

初夏の先付　Early summer appetizer

季節の懐石料理をこだわりの器で

ご提供する食事は、旬の素材をふんだんに使った懐石料理です。最初に料理長にお願いしたのは、つくり置きを機械的に出すような"団体料理"にはしたくないということでした。熱いものはアツアツで、冷たいものはキンと冷えた状態で。美味しさのタイミングを損なわず味わっていただきたいのです。しかもゆっくり寛いでいただくためにお部屋出しです。それを実現するには調理場と客室の距離が近くなければなりません。オープン間際になって設計を変更し、各フロアに最後の仕上げができる小さな厨房をつくりました。とにかく納得いくものをお出ししたい。その一念でした。

毎月月替わりのメニューはすべて試食し、盛り付けや器選びまでとことんこだわりました。たとえば朝食の海苔ひとつとっても、木炭を入れた「焙炉(ほいろ)」をテーブルにご用意し、その場で軽くあぶってパリパリになったところを召し上がっていただくという具合です。お着き菓子は、茶事に詳しい和菓子店から毎朝届く生菓子。おやすみ前のお茶の時間は、オリジナルの小箱入りの豆菓子をご用意します。食を通じて、丁寧で行き届いたおもてなしの心をお伝えできれば嬉しいの一心でした。

秋の八寸　Autumn dishes

Seasonal traditional cuisine, served on carefully chosen dishes

We offer traditional cuisine, using plentiful ingredients in season.

My first request to the chef was to avoid conventional "tour group" style serving, in which many dishes are made in advance and served to the guests mechanically. Hot dishes should be piping hot, cold dishes should be refreshingly cold. I wanted our guests to have food at the height of taste. Moreover, we would serve guests in their rooms, so they could relax. To realize these goals, the kitchen would have to be near the guest rooms. Just before we opened, I changed the design and installed a small kitchen on each guest floor where final food prep could be carried out. I was determined to give my guests what I would want for myself.

I oversaw every aspect of the food service, sampling everything in the monthly menu rotation, the way the food was plated, and the dishes it was served on. For example, I wanted to ensure that guests could enjoy their single sheet of nori, so I had small charcoal grills box placed on the tables to allow guests to lightly toast their nori until it was crisp and dry. Side sweets were delivered each morning by a Japanese sweets shop familiar with the tea ceremony. For teatime before bed, we prepared original small boxes containing tiny sweets.

I was devoted to ensuring that we conveyed a genuine spirit of hospitality in every aspect of the food we served.

「あじさい」の縁側から庭をのぞむ
Looking into the garden from the porch of Ajisai

花、花、花……

玄関を一歩入ると、お香で焚いた花の香りが漂います。そして、ご案内するお部屋には、「あじさい」「りんどう」「牡丹」「鈴蘭」……など、花の名前をつけました。「花」の字がつく屋号に恥じぬよう、花にまつわることを大切にしてきたのです。

館内には四季折々のいけ花を絶やすことはありません。小さな一輪挿しを含めると、全部で200カ所近くになるでしょうか。花専任の従業員が2人いますが、水を替えるだけでもてんてこ舞いです。

創業したばかりの頃は、私の思いが伝わらないこともありました。しばらく外出して戻ってみると、ロビーに「ここはベルサイユ宮殿？」と見まごうばかりのピンクのバラの花がどっさりいけてあるのです。確かに華やかではあるのですが、やはり和を基調とした空間には似合いません。

たとえば端午の節句には、大きな鉢に気高く咲く菖蒲の花など、花あしらいにも、日本の季節と風土の素晴らしさを感じていただきたい。「強羅花壇」の花にはそんな思いが込められています。

074

大浴場にわたる廊下　　Corridor connecting communal baths

山をのぞむ離れ「泉心」の露天風呂
Open-air bath at Senshin overlooking the mountains

Flowers, flowers, flowers!

As you step through the entrance, the aroma of flower-scented incense wafts through the air. Your room will be named after a flower—Hydrangea, Gentian, Peony, Lily and the like.

With Japanese "flower" (ka) featured in the name of the inn, I have always paid special attention to anything related to flowers.

Seasonal flower arrangements are an integral part of our interiors. If we count all the small vases holding a single flower, I would guess that flowers are displayed in close to two hundred locations throughout the inn. Two of our employees handle nothing but the flowers; watering alone keeps them on their feet all day.

Shortly after we opened, some of my concepts didn't come across as clearly as I intended. Once, after a brief absence, I returned to the lobby and was greeted by an overwhelming display of pink roses, so grand that I wondered if I had stepped into the Palace of Versailles. The roses were gorgeous of course, but they weren't at home in a Japanese setting.

For example, during the Iris Festival, we convey the splendor of the seasons and climate with majestic irises and other flowers arranged in large vases. This is what we aim to achieve with the flowers of Gora Kadan.

メイド・イン・ジャパン！

とにかく「日本」のものにこだわりました。

たとえば、ミネラルウォーターなら、『エヴィアン』ではなく「富士の水」。お風呂でお使いいただくシャンプーも、当時はまだ珍しかったヒノキの香りのオーガニックなものを特注でつくっていただきました。

洗面所のアメニティは、日本のブランド『福美水』や『SENSAI』のスキンケア製品をご用意しています。『福美水』は、ヨモギやクマザサ、シラカバなどの和漢植物が配合された化粧水で、私も使っていますが、驚くほど全身すべすべになります。海外のお客様のなかには、「強羅花壇で使って気に入ったから」と、わざわざ本社まで買いに行かれた方もいたそうです。

『SENSAI』は、日本発ながらまず海外で販売スタートされたラグジュアリーブランドで、こちらも「強羅花壇で知った」というお客様からの問い合わせが多いそうです。

お客様に安心してお使いいただけるもの、心地いいもの、とあちこち探し回りまし

た。その結果、たどり着いたのは、やはり日本のものだったのです。

タオルも、すべてのお部屋でというわけにはいかないのですが、名産地・今治で出合った「イケウチオーガニック」のものをそろえました。

ただタオルはいくらよいものでも、業務用クリーニングを繰り返せば、せっかくの風合いや肌触りが損なわれてしまいます。理想は自分のところで専用の洗濯工場を持つことですが、さすがにそれはこだわり過ぎでしょうか。

売店に置く食品や工芸品などのお土産物も、すべて自分自身で選びました。全国各地に散らばる歴史ある銘品、隠れた逸品。そんなものを求めて、どの地を訪れても

「うちの売店でご紹介できるものはないかしら」と探してしまいます。

静岡県の「土炎手窯（どえんでがま）」（故人）の陶芸作品もそうでした。東京のデパートの期間限定ショップで、ひと目で気に入りご連絡をしたのがはじまりで、売店の大人気商品となりました。そして、売店一のベストセラーは、嬉しいことに、なんと私自身がデザインした浴衣、帯、タビックス、草履の4点セットです。

「そんなことまでして、たいへんですね」とよく言われます。でも、好きなことですのでまったく苦ではありませんでした。毎日、毎日、「強羅花壇」のことばかり考え、夢中になって駆け抜けた日々でした。

ゆったりとした一般客室　Spacious bedroom

Made in Japan!

I wanted everything to be about Japan.

Mineral water—Evian? No. Mt. Fuji Natural Mineral Water. I couldn't find a shampoo I could approve for the guest baths, so I had one formulated—organic and scented with Japanese cypress. At the time, such shampoos were rare at Japanese inns.

We use Japanese-made amenities in the baths, such as Fukubisui and SENSAI skin care products. Fukubisui lotion contains Chinese and Japanese herbs like mugwort, bamboo grass, and white birch. I use it myself, and I'm surprised how smooth it leaves my skin. I understand that certain guests have even visited the company's headquarters to purchase these products after having first experienced them at Gora Kadan.

Despite being a Japanese luxury brand, SENSAI was launched in Europe. Again, many of our guests have said they encountered it for the first time when staying with us.

I spent a great deal of time searching for products that our guests can use with peace of mind, products that will make them comfortable. And somehow, I always found that what I was looking for is made in Japan.

Where we can, we equip our guest rooms with Ikeuchi Organic towels, which I discovered in Imabari, which is famous for towels.

広々としたプール&ジャグジー　Spacious swimming pool & jacuzzi

エステサロンでくつろぐ　Relaxing at the esthetic salon

Of course, no matter the quality of the towel, with repeated commercial cleaning, the original texture and feel will be lost. While it is ideal to have an in-house laundry, its feasibility could be limited.

I also personally selected all of the food and craft objects sold in our inn shop. There are historic and hidden treasures scattered all over Japan. Whenever I travel, I actively look for new ideas or products that could be introduced to our shop.

Works by Doende-gama of Shizuoka are one example. I first saw them at a limited-time shop in a Tokyo department store and was immediately taken with them; today they are very popular items in our shop. And I'm pleased to say that the best-selling product in the shop is the bundle consisting of a robe, a sash, tabi socks, and zori sandals, all of my own design.

"That sounds like a lot of effort," I was often told. But it was something I enjoyed, so it was no effort at all. Each day, Gora Kadan was constantly on my mind, and time seemed to pass by in the blink of an eye.

着物に込めたおもてなしの心

着物を着たのは、七五三のお宮参りのときが最初で最後。そんな私が、女将になって、はじめて着物の世界を知りました。

何百種類もある日本の伝統色の、なんと美しいことでしょう！　着物と帯、帯締めと帯揚げなど、色合わせは無限に広がり、その組み合わせをあれこれ考えるだけでワクワクと楽しくて、すっかりこの世界にはまってしまいました。

とはいえ、女将はあくまでもお客様の引き立て役です。出過ぎることなく、自分は、無地か小紋の地味な着物を選ぶことを心がけていました。

仲居さんたちも全員着物ですが、「強羅花壇」では、季節によって色や素材を変えるのはもちろん、朝と夕方でもそれぞれ違う色柄のものに着替えます。夕刻からは、お出迎えに備えてシックな色調に。朝の時間帯は少し爽やかに。

そこまでやるのは業界でも珍しいことですが、従業員の装いもまた旅館の一部です。お客様は、従業員の着物の違いなど気づかないかもしれません。でも、気づかれないところこそ、手を抜きたくありませんでした。たとえ小さなこだわりでも、その一

086

つひとつが積み重なって、おもてなしの心に連なるのです。

仲居さんの着物は、すべて私が呉服店で色柄を選び、反物から染めてもらいました。小物の色合わせも自分で決めて指示を出しました。

新人はたいへんだったと思います。ただでさえ慣れない着物なのに、一日に2度も着替えをさせられて。しかもワンタッチ帯など一切使わず、正式な手順通りに自分で着つけをしなければならないのです。

偉そうなことを言っても、私自身、なんとか着物姿がさまになるまでには3年くらいかかりました。

ただ、きちんと着物を着ると、歩き方や立ち居振る舞いがきれいになります。気持ちもシャンと引きしまります。

ここを卒業していった元仲居さんのなかには、「あのとき苦労して学んだことが、今では私の財産です」と言ってくれる人もいます。厳しいことも言いましたが、ついてきてくれたみんなには感謝の気持ちでいっぱいです。

閑院宮の別荘は「懐石料理 花壇」として使われている
Prince Kan'in no Miya's villa now welcomes guests as Kaiseki Restaurant Kadan

I chose the colors and patterns for the staff kimonos and had the fabric dyed accordingly. I also selected the accessory color scheme and had them custom-made to order.

This must have been hard on our new staff, who are not only unused to kimonos, but are required to change into them twice a day. Naturally we do not use "one-touch" sashes or other conveniences. Each staff member has to dress herself in the correct manner without any assistance.

I can't say I was any better at wearing a kimono than my staff. It took me about three years to get to the point where I could wear one properly.

Still, when you know how to wear a kimono, you become mindful of your movements and posture, cultivating a sense of focus and grace.

Some of our staff alumni have told me, "What I learned then under pressure is now an asset for me." I may have been tough on them at times, but I am deeply grateful to everyone who remainded steadfast by my side.

Hospitality in kimono

My first and last experience of wearing a kimono as a child was while visiting a shrine as a young girl. When I became the proprietor of an inn, I learned about the real world of kimono.

How beautiful those hundreds of traditional Japanese colors are!

The possibilities for color matching between kimono, obi, and accessories are endless. Just thinking about the different combinations is exciting and fun. I've become completely absorbed by this world.

Still, the proprietor's role is to be a foil for the guests. As such, I tried not to be too conspicuous, and to limit myself to plain or small-patterned, subdued kimonos.

The staff also wear kimonos, but at Gora Kadan, they change their kimono not only according to the season, but also morning and evening.

Morning kimonos are somewhat lively. In the late afternoon, when receiving guests, the staff switch to more subdued, elegant colors.

It may be unusual for an inn to go that far, but our staff attire is part of the guest experience.

Guests may not notice that the staff kimonos change. Still, I did not want to cut corners just because something was unlikely to be noticed. Attention to even small details adds up and contributes to the spirit of hospitality.

すべてはお客様に喜んでいただくため

私が大切にしていたおもてなしの基本は、まず掃除でした。

たとえば、表の門をくぐって玄関に至るアプローチ。そこには雑草一本、小さなゴミ一つ許されません。ピンセットで取るくらいの気持ちで取り組みました。打ち水もそうですが、そもそも玄関をきれいにすることは、場を浄めることにつながります。凜として張りつめた美しさを保つことで、お客様に心からの歓迎の意をお伝えすることができるのです。

それから、お客様の車を洗っておくのも、他にはない、うちならではのおもてなしの一つでした。滞在を楽しんでくださったお客様には、ピカピカの車でお帰りいただきたかったからです。夏はカンカン照りの日差しのなか、冬は小雪がちらつくなか、フロントスタッフたちは嫌な顔ひとつせず、よくやってくれました。

すべてはお客様に喜んでいただくため。従業員のそんな心意気があったからこそ、みなさまに評価していただける〝強羅花壇らしさ〟が生まれたのだと信じています。

離れ・「残月」のお風呂から花を楽しむ
Enjoying blossoms from the bath at Zangetsu

Everything we do is to please our guests

The first basic principle of hospitality that I valued was cleanliness.

For example, not a single weed or tiny piece of trash was allowed along the approach from the front gate to the entrance. We worked with the utmost care to remove even a single weed with tweezers.

Keeping the entrance beautiful also purifies the space. Maintaining a dignified, mindful beauty conveys a heartfelt welcome to guests.

Washing the guests' cars was another form of hospitality found only at Gora Kadan. I wanted guests to leave in a sparkling-clean car after enjoying their stay. Under a hot sun in summer or amid snow flurries in winter, I could rely on our reception staff to always cheerfully carry out this task.

Everything we did was to please our guests. I am convinced that it is precisely because our staff were committed to achieving this that Gora Kadan became renowned as the epitome of hospitality.

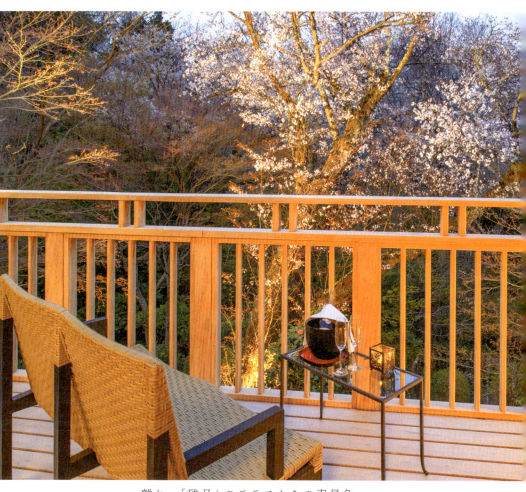

離れ・「残月」のテラスからの春景色
Spring scenery from the terrace of Zangetsu

おもてなしとは

ある日、2人の男の子を連れたアメリカ人のご夫妻がチェックインされました。何気ない会話のなかで、「子どもたちに、ぜひ日本の文化を教えたいのです」とおっしゃったのが印象的でした。

私たちが何かをお教えするなど、おこがましい話です。ですが、スタッフのちょっとした立ち居振る舞いや礼儀、心配りなどのおもてなしの姿勢から、小さなお子さまにも何かを感じていただけることもあるでしょう。

担当の仲居さんは、まだ入社したての新人で少し不安でしたが、「精一杯喜んでいただいてね」と、背中を押してお客様のところへ向かわせました。

そして三泊の滞在を終え、いよいよチェックアウトの朝。

ご夫妻は「子どもたちを連れてきて本当によかった」と涙ながらにおっしゃってくださいました。仲居さんは、ただ、お客様のために一所懸命尽くしただけでしょう。でも、それをこんなに喜んでいただけたのですから、私も本当に嬉しく感激でした。

最後の最後まで手を振ってくださるご一家を見送りながら、担当した子は立ち尽くし

096

たままわんわん泣いていました。

そんな彼女も、今では結婚してお母さんです。ここで経験し学んだことが、きっと何かのかたちで役立っていることでしょう。

日本語には「徳を積む」という言葉があります。人に親切にしたり、善い行いを重ねるということです。お客様に喜んでいただくというおもてなしの仕事は、まさに徳を積むことになるのではないでしょうか。

決して見返りを求めているわけではありません。ですが、相手に喜んでもらえばもらうほど自分にも喜びが返ってきて、人間的にも成長できるのです。こんなにありがたいことはありません。

仲居さんのなかには、70歳過ぎたベテランもいます。「私、もうトシですから」などと言いながらも、お客様からご指名をいただくと、がぜんやる気がわいて自然に体が動くのだと笑っています。

おもてなしは一方的に「してあげる」ことではなく、「させていただく」喜びややりがいに満ちています。彼女もまた、そんなやりがいを知る一人なのです。

月見台から柱廊をのぞむ　Admiring the colonnade from the moon viewing platform

Hospitality accumulates

One day an American couple with two young boys checked in.

As I was chatting with them, I was surprised when one said, "We want our children to learn about Japanese culture."

I felt it would be presumptuous to think we could teach them.

Still, there might well be something in the hospitality of our staff—their movements and demeanor, their courtesy and small kindnesses to guests—that might convey itself to small children.

The girl I assigned to look after the family had just joined us. I questioned whether she was the right fit for the task, but I encouraged her with a gentle push telling her to do her best to make them happy.

The morning after their three-night stay, the family was checking out.

The husband and wife said tearfully, "We're so glad we brought the children." The staff member I assigned had simply done her best to ensure they were happy, but she evidently succeeded so well that I was thoroughly delighted. As their car drove away, the family went on waving goodbye to us until they were out of sight, and the girl who had looked after them stood there weeping.

That same girl is now married, with children. I am

フィットネスジムで汗を流す
Working up a sweat at the fitness center

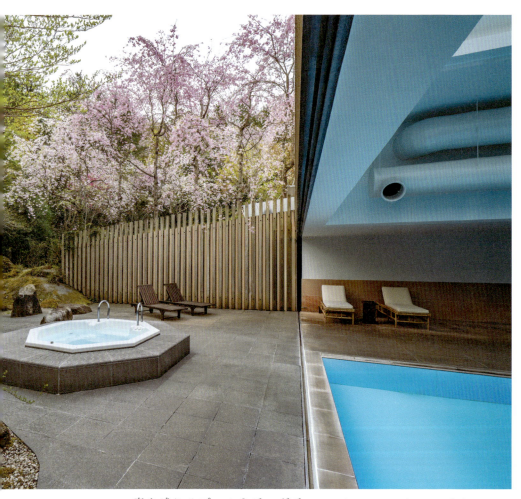

春を感じるプール&ジャグジー　Pool & jacuzzi with a spring feeling

confident that she is applying the experiences and lessons she gained during her time with us to good use.

There is an expression in Japanese, "accumulate virtue." It refers to being kind to people and doing good things for them again and again over time. I believe that the work of hospitality, of making guests happy, is a perfect example of accumulating virtue.

Virtue does not expect anything in return. But the more you make others happy, the more their happiness returns to you, and you grow as a person. There is nothing more precious than this.

One of our staff is a veteran who is over 70. "I'm over the hill," she sometimes says, but when a guest requests her specifically, she can't help but smile as she watches her motivation soar and sees how effortlessly she thrives.

Hospitality does not consist of one-way acts of service. It is full of the joy and fulfillment that comes from being given the opportunity to serve. Our senior staff member is someone who understands this.

人の笑顔を見ることが嬉しくて……

「これまでまったく畑違いの仕事をしてきたのに、どうして女将さん業ができたのですか?」と聞かれて、ハッと気づいたことがありました。

考えてみれば、私は、昔から人をおもてなしするのが好きだったのです。

子どもの頃から、友だちが遊びにくると張り切ってケーキを焼いたり、部屋に花を飾ったりしたものです。

結婚してすぐの頃には、夫の友人や仕事仲間がよく家に寄ってくださり、その度に嬉々として台所に立ちました。人が喜ぶ顔を見ると嬉しくなるのです。

「強羅花壇」をはじめてからは、「ここでプロポーズしたい」というお客様に、いろいろなアイディアをご提案したり、「次は京都へ行く」と聞けば現地のおすすめレストランを予約してさしあげることもありました。お客様と一緒にあたりを散策したり、箱根の名所や美術館をご案内するのも楽しい時間でした。

おもてなしといえば、もう一つ忘れられないのが、イタリア留学時代の体験です。

学生ですからアパート式の学生寮を友人とシェアしていました。食べるものも倹約

104

し、冬は底冷えする寒さのなか、暖房器具もほとんどなく震える生活でした。

そんなとき、「台所のかまどに火を焚いたから、暖まりにおいで」と声をかけてくれたのがお隣の奥さんでした。ご主人がドイツに出稼ぎに行っているそうで、歯科衛生士のお嬢さんと2人暮らし。決して豊かな生活ではありません。

行くと、かまどにはペントラという小さなお鍋がかかっていて、トマトソースがグツグツと煮えていました。

「ごはん食べた？」「いえ、まだです……」

すると、奥さんは、そのトマトソースでパスタをつくってくれました。2人分しかないソースを4人分のパスタと和えれば、味は薄くなってしまいます。それでも、私たちに分け与えてくれたのです。我がままに育った私ですが、人の優しさがどんなに心に響くかを知りました。志なかばで呼び戻されてしまいましたが、イタリアへ行ったのは決して無駄ではありませんでした。

後に自分がこうしておもてなしをさせていただく立場になって、つくづく思います。自分がしてきたことは一つひとつバラバラに見えて、すべてはつながっていたのだなと。

105

プールの屋根からながめる柱廊　　Gallery viewed from the pool roof

One cold day, the lady next door said to me, "I'm cooking on the stove. Why don't you come in and warm up?" Her husband was away working in Germany, and she was living with her daughter, who was a dental technician. It was no easy feat for them to get by.

So we went next door to her kitchen. She had a small pot on the stove with tomato sauce bubbling away.

"Have you eaten?" she asked, and I confessed that we hadn't.

At this, she made pasta for us. There was only enough sauce for two people, so with four portions, the flavor was diluted, nevertheless, she generously shared it with us. Having been raised with everything I could ever want, I realized how much a person's act of kindness can resonate.

Although I had to cut my studies short, my time in Italy was incredibly worthwhile.

Eventually, offering hospitality became my role and looking back, I now see how everything I've done has been interconnected.

When I see our guests smiling, I can't help but be pleased

Someone once asked me, "How did you manage to start running an inn without any prior experience?" The question made me suddenly realize something.

It occurred to me that in fact, I have always enjoyed providing people with hospitality. As a child, if a friend came to visit I would go all out and do things like bake a cake, or decorate my room with flowers.

Early in my marriage, friends and work colleagues of my husband would often drop by, and I would happily go to work making something in the kitchen. It makes me happy to see others happy.

After I launched Gora Kadan, a guest might say "I want to propose to my partner while we're here," and I would help them think of ways to make that special. "I'm going to Kyoto after my stay here," I would hear someone say, and I would suggest a restaurant and make reservations for them. I took walks in the vicinity with guests, or showed them to famous spots or museums in Hakone. I always enjoyed the time spent.

Speaking of hospitality, I have an unforgettable memory from my time in Italy.

As a student, I was sharing a apartment with a friend. We didn't have much to spend on food; in winter, the domitory apartment was freezing, and we shivered without hardly any heating.

春の離れ・「花香」の入り口　Entrance to Kakou in spring

人から人へ評判が伝わって

宣伝らしい宣伝は、何もしてきませんでした。

部屋に露天風呂がついているスタイルが目新しかったのでしょう。女性誌や旅行雑誌もこぞって取り上げてくださいました。おかげさまで徐々に新生〝花壇〟が認知されていきました。

そのうち海外からのお客様も増えました。今のようにインターネットもない時代です。うちを探し当ててくださったのは、圧倒的に口コミの力のおかげでした。

あるとき、ガイドブックを手にした外国人のお客さまがいらっしゃいました。ふと見ると、そこには『150 Hotels You Need to Visit Before You Die（死ぬまでに泊まるべき150の宿）』とあります。タイトルのユニークさに思わず笑ってしまいましたが、ここにもどなたかうちのお客様が良いコメントを投稿してくださったのでしょう。

人から人へ直接伝わっていくことのありがたさが身にしみました。

一つひとつの出会いが宝ものです

女将として鍛錬を積んだわけでもなく、接客業にも無縁だった私が、長きにわたりこの「強羅花壇」でお客様をお迎えしてきました。

自分が至らないばかりにご迷惑をおかけして、落ち込むこともありました。このような私について来てくれた多くの従業員たちには、心より感謝しています。つらいことや大変だったこともたくさんあったはずです。しかし、思い出すのは楽しかった思い出ばかりです。お客様の笑顔や温かさ、かけていただいた優しい言葉……どんな場面を切り取ってみても、すべてはお金には換えられない大きな喜びでした。旅館の女将とお客様という立場を超えて、心と心の交流をさせていただけました。

今でも世界中からご連絡をくださる方もたくさんいらっしゃいます。お食事をご一緒したり、別荘づくりやインテリアなどのご相談を受けることもあります。それは人脈と呼ばれるようなビジネスライクなものではありません。

一つひとつの出会いが、私の人生でかけがえのない宝ものなのです。それもすべてこの「強羅花壇」があったからこそだと確信しています。

春の夜半に別邸の庭をのぞむ　Looking into the villa garden in the small hours of spring night

Reputation is transmitted from person to person

I never did anything that could be called promotion.

Private open-air baths for guests was a new concept that received blanket coverage in women's magazines and travel magazines. All this attention drove awareness of the new inn.

We soon started receiving more international guests as well. There was no Internet in those days. Instead, it was overwhelmingly the power of word of mouth that enabled these guests to find us.

Once a foreign guest arrived with a guidebook in hand. When I glanced at the cover, I saw that the title was *150 Hotels You Need to Visit Before You Die*. I couldn't help laughing at the unique title, but my guess is that if we were listed there, it was because of comments from our guests.

I believe that real promotion is information that travels directly from person to person. I am deeply grateful for this support.

Each encounter is precious

Although I had no formal training in inn management or in the hospitality industry, I have welcomed guests at Gora Kadan for many years.

My guests were patient with my shortcomings, which at times weighed heavily on me. I am deeply grateful to the dedicated staff members who stayed by my side for so long.

Along the way there must have been many painful and difficult challenges, yet all of my memories are happy ones—the smiling faces and warmth of the guests, the kind things they said...

Each memory I cherish fills me with great joy and it is something I wouldn't trade for all the money in the world. I transcended the roles of inn proprietor and guest and engaged in heart-to-heart communication.

I continue to receive many communications from people around the world. I share meals with them, or offer advice on constructing a villa or decorating interiors. These are not sterile, businesslike exchanges, but rather meaningful engaged interactions.

Every one of my encounters with people has been a precious treasure. Gora Kadan made them all possible.

大浴場で強羅の巨石をながめる
Looking out over Gora's large rocks from the communal baths

日本の「おもてなし」の極美を堪能する時間

世界中の楽園を探し、撮影旅をして来ました。タヒチ、ハワイ、モルディブなどの南国のリゾート。さらにインド、ヒマラヤ、モロッコからヨーロッパ、アジア諸国まで。その土地でも一流と称されるホテルを体験して来ました。

三十代になるまでは海外へ行くことが多かったのですが、それ以降は日本を旅することが増えました。ある程度の年齢になり、日本の美しさが表面でなく、心で理解できるようになって、それを写真に収めることができました。

世界を周り、日本を巡って、出合ったのが箱根の「強羅花壇」です。

初めて訪れたときは、名旅館の名前にいささか緊張しました。でも、その緊張はすぐにほぐれることになりました。「ああ、これが日本のおもてなしなのだ」と、心から癒される気分になったのです。

漆黒のエレベーターに乗ったときの芳しい香り。世界でも、こんなささやかで心優しい、もてなしは体験できません。さらに素晴らしいのは進化をやめないこと。名旅館でありながら変化を続ける「強羅花壇」には、いつも新しい発見があり、ときめきがあります。

三好和義（写真家）

夕暮れどきの家族風呂　Family baths at sunset

存在感がある庭の石　　Garden stone with a commanding presence

Experiencing the ultimate in Japanese hospitality

I've traveled the globe as a photographer, searching for paradise. I've visited tropical resorts—Tahiti, Hawaii, the Maldives. I've journeyed to India and the Himalayas, traveled from Morocco to Europe to the countries of Asia. And along the way, I've experienced many high-end hotels.

Until my thirties, I spent much of my time abroad. But after thirty, I spent more time in Japan. Once I reached a certain age, I began to grasp Japan's beauty—not superficially, but from the heart. That allowed me to capture it in photographs.

I circled the globe, wandered Japan, and found Gora Kadan in Hakone.

On my first visit, its reputation had preceded it, and I was a bit nervous. But all my tension quickly melted. "This is true Japanese hospitality," I thought, and I felt it healing my heart.

The sweet fragrance when I boarded the jet-black elevator! Nowhere else in the world can you experience hospitality with such unassuming, heartfelt warmth. Even more wonderful is that it never stops evolving. At Gora Kadan, that inn of inns, ever-changing, there is always the new to discover and delight.

Kazuyoshi Miyoshi
Photographer

あとがき

春は枝垂桜が見ごろを迎え、夏は心地よい風が緑を揺らす。山装う錦秋の季節や薄っすらと積もる冬の雪景色を露天風呂から眺める……。四季折々の自然の移ろいを愉しめる「強羅花壇」の様子を最初から撮り続けていただいたのは、日本を代表する写真家の三好和義先生です。数十年にわたる撮影の作品を本書に提供いただき誠にありがとうございます。

そして、本書刊行にご協力いただいたすべての方々にあらためてお礼申し上げます。私と同じ時期にキャリアをスタートさせ、今や世界で活躍するアンテプリマのクリエイティブ・ディレクターの荻野いづみさんをはじめ、何十年ものおつき合いの友人たちにはいつも励ましていただきました。また「強羅花壇」が最高のおもてなしを提供できるよう尽力していただいたスタッフ、そしてさまざまな協力会社の皆様に深く感謝申し上げます。

最後に「強羅花壇」を愛し、今なおご利用いただいている世界中のお客様に心の深いところよりお礼申し上げます。

藤本三和子

柱廊の横にある水路　Waterway beside the gallery

Afterword

In spring, a weeping cherry tree shows off its blossoms. In summer, cooling breezes make the foliage sway. The view from an open-air bath toward mountains clad in autumn crimson, a winter scene with a light dusting of snow... From the beginning, Kazuyoshi Miyoshi, one of Japan's greatest photographers, has been recording the changing face of Gora Kadan through the seasons. I extend my profound gratitude to him for granting permission to include his photographic works, captured over the decades, in this book.

Let me also thank once again all those who contributed to the publication of this book. My heartfelt appreciation goes to the many friends who have consistently offered their encouragement and support over the decades, beginning with Izumi Ogino, who began her career around the same time I did, and who is today the Creative Director at the fashion icon ANTEPRIMA Limited. I will forever be indebted to our staff members and partner companies who continue working tirelessly so that Gora Kadan can offer unsurpassed hospitality.

Finally, I wish to convey my deepest gratitude to those guests all over the world who love Gora Kadan and keep coming back.

Miwako Fujimoto

本文デザイン　有限会社レゾナ

編集協力　金原みはる

英訳　株式会社TENインターナショナル

藤本三和子（ふじもと・みわこ）

「強羅花壇」元女将。東京生まれ。イタリア語の通訳やイタリア関係の仕事に従事した後、1989年、新生「強羅花壇」をオープンさせ日本を代表する旅館に育て上げる。海外にアンテナを張り、建築や芸術に対する知見を深め、「強羅花壇」にその美学を凝縮させたといわれる。

三好和義（みよし・かずよし）

写真家。1958年、徳島市生まれ。85年にデビュー写真集『RAKUEN』を出版、この作品で木村伊兵衛写真賞を当時最年少で受賞する。以降、「楽園」をテーマに撮影を続け、日本の四季や伝統美にも「楽園」を見出し、日本の世界遺産まで幅広く撮影。仏像から日本の世界遺産まで幅広く撮影。

強羅花壇ものがたり

2025年3月28日　第1版第1刷発行

著　者　藤本三和子
写　真　三好和義
発行者　村上雅基
発行所　株式会社PHP研究所
　　　　京都本部　〒601-8411　京都市南区西九条北ノ内町11
　　　　　　　　　教育企画部　☎075-681-5040（編集）
　　　　東京本部　〒135-8137　江東区豊洲5-6-52
　　　　　　　　　普及部　☎03-3520-9630（販売）
　　　　PHP INTERFACE　https://www.php.co.jp/

組　版　有限会社レゾナ
印刷所
製本所　TOPPANクロレ株式会社

©Miwako Fujimoto & Kazuyoshi Miyoshi 2025 Printed in Japan
ISBN978-4-569-85897-5

※本書の無断複製（コピー・スキャン・デジタル化等）は著作権法で認められた場合を除き、禁じられています。また、本書を代行業者等に依頼してスキャンやデジタル化することは、いかなる場合でも認められておりません。
※落丁、乱丁本の場合は弊社制作管理部（☎03-3520-9626）へご連絡ください。送料弊社負担にてお取り替えいたします。